LATINA CHRISTIANA

An Introduction to Christian Latin

BOOK I

STUDENT BOOK

by Cheryl Lowe

CLASSICAL TRIVIUM CORE SERIES

LATINA CHRISTIANA: STUDENT BOOK I
© 1998, 2000, 2002
Third Edition, Memoria Press
ISBN #: 1-930953-02-X

4103 Bishop Lane, Louisville, KY 40218
www.memoriapress.com

Printed in the USA, 08-04

Latin is a language that has a respect unequaled by any other language. It brings to mind academic excellence, accomplishment, culture, and tradition. When you tell people you are studying Latin at such a young age, they will probably be amazed and impressed.

I hope you want to be successful in your study of Latin and I will tell you how. In your history lessons, you will learn about a little village in Italy that went on to conquer all of Italy and eventually the whole Mediterranean world. This little village, of course, was Rome. How did Rome do what older, richer, and more advanced cities could not do? Rome had patience and perseverance. Rome was steady and consistent, not just for a day, a month, or a year, but for centuries! The key to success is steady, consistent work that perseveres, even when the task is difficult.

If you will study Latin a little every day, then you will conquer Latin. If you try to learn Latin once a week or just before a test, then Latin will conquer you. Like the tortoise that beat the hare, the race goes not to the swift but to the strong. By persevering in Latin you will develop the "mental strength" you need to accomplish greater and even more difficult tasks.

I hope you like Latin. It is intriguing, much like a challenging game. Like any challenge, it spurs you on to greater energy and determination. When you conquer Latin grammar you will be like the Romans. You will be ready to go out and conquer the world!

Cheryl Lowe, *Magistra*

PRONUNCIATION RULES

The Alphabet

The Latin alphabet has no "w". Words with "y" are of Greek origin.

Vowels

In Christian Latin vowels are usually long.

Vowel	Long	Example
a	'father' (ah)	ad, mater
e	'they' (ay)	me, video
i	'machine' (ee)	video, qui
o	'no' (oh)	porta, omnis
u	'rule' (oo)	cum, sumus

Sometimes the vowels **e** and **i** tend toward the short vowel sounds ('Ed','it') as in 'mensa' and 'et'.

Diphthongs and digraphs

Digraph	Pronunciation	Example
ae } oe }	like *e* in 'they' (ay)	saepe, praemium, proelium

Diphthong		
au	like *ou* in out (ow)	laudo, nauta

Consonants

Most of the consonants are pronounced as in English, with the following exceptions.

Consonant	Pronunciation	Examples
c	before *e, i, ae, oe* like *ch* in 'charity'	decem, cibus caelum
c	before other letters, hard *c* as in 'cut'	clamo, culpa
g	soft before *e, i, ae, oe* as in 'gym'	regina, gemini
g	hard before other letters as in 'go'	gratia, fuga
gn	like *gn* as in 'lasagna'	pugno, regnum
j	like *y* as in 'yet'	judico, Jesus
s	like *s* as in 'sing' (never like *z*)	tres, mensa
sc	like sh	discipulus
t	when followed by *i* and a vowel, like *tsee*	gratia, tertius nuntius

In words of three or more syllables, the accent mark indicates the stressed syllable. It is not necessary for the student to learn the location of the accent mark, or to copy it when writing Latin.

Table of *CONTENTS*

Latin I
Lessons

LESSON I

Latin Saying

Ora et labora.   Pray and work.

> — St. Benedict

Vocabulary

1. **amo**   I love

2. **porto**   I carry

3. **laudo**   I praise

4. **oro**   I pray

5. **labóro**   I work

Grammar Forms

First Conjugation

amo	amámus
amas	amátis
amat	amant

A. Translation

1. Salve, magistra (p.74) _____

2. Ora et labora. _____

3. laudo _____

4. oro _____

B. Grammar

1. A verb is a word that shows _____ .

2. The letter 'o' at the end of a Latin verb stands for the pronoun _____ .

3. A _____ is included in every Latin verb.

C. Derivatives. Complete these sentences with derivatives you have learned in class.

1. Something light enough to carry is _____ . **(porto)**

2. Scientists perform experiments in a _____ . **(laboro)**
   Advanced Derivatives
3. Someone who is a good public speaker is an _____ . **(oro)**

4. Something that is worthy to be praised is _____ . **(laudo)**

LESSON II

Latin Saying

Mater Italiae — Roma   The mother of Italy — Rome

Vocabulary

1.	**Roma**	Rome
2.	**Itália**	Italy
3.	**glória**	glory
4.	**vita**	life
5.	**aqua**	water
6.	**memória**	memory
7.	**victória**	victory
8.	**návigo**	I sail
9.	**paro**	I prepare
10.	**specto**	I look at

Grammar Forms

Verb Personal Endings

-o	**-mus**
-s	**-tis**
-t	**-nt**

A. Translation

1. Salvete, discipuli (p.74) _____

2. Mater Italiae — Roma _____

3. Ora et labora. _____

4. Meum praenomen est (p.74) _____

B. Grammar

1. A noun is a word that names a _____,_____,_____.

2. A pronoun takes the place of a _____.

3. Write the English pronouns that correspond to these endings:

-o _____   -mus _____

-s _____   -tis _____

-t _____   -nt _____

C. Derivatives

1. The fish were swimming in the _____. **(aqua)**

2. The _____ cheered their team. **(specto)**

3. Rome was always _____ over her enemies. **(victoria)**

4. Careful _____ usually leads to success. **(paro)**

5. _____ contribute to good health. **(vita)**

Advanced Derivatives

6. Rome built many _____to carry water to the cities. **(aqua)**

7. The river was difficult to _____. **(navigo)**

LESSON III

Latin Saying

Caelum et terra   Heaven and earth

Vocabulary

1. terra   land, earth
2. lingua   language
3. via   road, way
4. fortúna   fortune, chance
5. herba   plant, herb
6. nauta   sailor
7. Gállia   Gaul
8. clamo   I shout
9. voco   I call
10. súpero   I overcome, conquer

Grammar Forms

First Conjugation

	Singular	*Plural*
1st P.	**voco**	**vocámus**
2nd P.	**vocas**	**vocátis**
3rd P.	**vocat**	**vocant**

A. Translation

1. Mater Italiae — Roma _____

2. Pray and work. _____

3. Meum praenomen est _____

4. Hello, teacher _____

B. Grammar

1. *Singular* means _____ in number.

2. _____ means more than one.

3. The _____ person is the person speaking.

4. The _____ is the person spoken to.

5. The _____ person is the person spoken about.

6. Conjugate *laudo* and give the English meanings.

_____ _____ _____ _____

_____ _____ _____ _____

_____ _____ _____ _____

C. Circle the personal endings of these verbs and translate.

superamus _____ paras _____

clamant _____ spectat _____

navigatis _____ vocamus _____

D. Derivatives

1. When the settlers moved west, they had to go through Indian _____. (**terra**)

2. You are _____ to be able to study Latin. (**fortuna**)

3. Latin study will make you a _____ student. (**supero**)

   Advanced Derivatives

4. The "_____ Dolorosa" is the Way of Sorrows that Christ walked to Calvary. (**via**)

5. The _____ was the name of the submarine in *20,000 Leagues Under the Sea.* (**nauta**)

6. He was bi-_____; he could speak two languages. (**lingua**)

LESSON IV

Latin Saying

E pluribus unum   One out of many
— motto of the United States

Vocabulary

1. **unus**   one
2. **duo**   two
3. **tres**   three
4. **quáttuor**   four
5. **quinque**   five
6. **sex**   six
7. **septem**   seven
8. **octo**   eight
9. **novem**   nine
10. **decem**   ten
11. **centum**   one hundred
12. **mille**   one thousand

Grammar Forms

Irregular verb *to be*

	S.	*Pl.*
1st P.	**sum**	**sumus**
2nd P.	**es**	**estis**
3rd P.	**est**	**sunt**

A. Translation

1. Pray and work.   _____

2. Quid est tuum praenomen ?(p.74) _____

3. Caelum et terra   _____

4. The mother of Italy—Rome   _____

5. Salvete amici Latinae (p. 74)   _____

B. Grammar

1. A verb is a word that shows action or _____.

2. The part of a Latin word that doesn't change is called the _____.

C. Circle the personal endings and translate.

1. sunt   _____   7. estis   _____

2. spectas   _____   8. clamo   _____

3. orat   _____   9. vocat   _____

4. paramus   _____   10. sumus   _____

5. amatis   _____   11. navigatis _____

6. laudant   _____   12. superant _____

D. Derivatives

1. How many years are there in a decade?   _____

2. How many years are there in a millenium?   _____

3. How many years are there in a century?   _____

4. How many singers are there in a duet?   _____

5. How many sides does an octagon have?   _____

6. How many musicians are there in a quartet?   _____

7. How many horns does a unicorn have?   _____

8. How many men did a Roman centurion command? _____

9. If a mother has quintuplets, how many babies does she have? _____

10. What Latin word do *unity* and *union* come from? _____

LESSON V

Latin Saying

Labor omnia vincit.
　—Virgil

Work conquers all.

Vocabulary

1.	**fémina**	woman
2.	**fília**	daughter
3.	**regína**	queen
4.	**mensa**	table
5.	**puélla**	girl
6.	**toga**	toga
7.	**pátria**	fatherland, country
8.	**adóro**	I adore
9.	**líbero**	I free
10.	**ámbulo**	I walk

Grammar Forms

First Declension

Singular	*Plural*
mensa	**mensae**
mensae	**mensárum**
mensae	**mensis**
mensam	**mensas**
mensa	**mensis**

A. Translation

1. E pluribus unum _____
2. Heaven and earth _____
3. Hello, friends of Latin _____
4. Meum praenomen est _____

B. Grammar

1. Adding the personal endings to a verb is called _____ a verb.
2. Adding case endings to a noun is called _____ a noun.
3. Conjugate these verbs and translate.

   a. adoro _____ _____ _____ _____

   _____ _____ _____ _____

   _____ _____ _____ _____

   b. ambulo _____ _____ _____ _____

   _____ _____ _____ _____

   _____ _____ _____ _____

C. Circle the personal endings and translate.

1. navigamus _____
2. ambulatis _____
3. liberant _____
4. laboras _____
5. parat _____
6. adoro _____
7. portatis _____
8. clamant _____
9. adorat _____
10. laudas _____
11. amamus _____
12. spectant _____

D. Derivatives

1. A _____ loves his country. (**patria**)
2. Christ _____ us from the power of sin. (**libero**)
3. He rode in an _____ because he could not walk. (**ambulo**)
4. Boys are masculine, while girls are _____. (**femina**)

Advanced Derivatives

5. She had _____ affection for her father. (**filia**)
6. We should express _____ for God during worship. (**adoro**)

REVIEW LESSON I

Vocabulary

Verbs

adoro	navigo
ambulo	oro
amo	paro
clamo	porto
laboro	specto
laudo	supero
libero	voco

Nouns

aqua	nauta
femina	patria
filia	puella
fortuna	regina
gloria	Roma
Gallia	terra
herba	toga
Italia	via
lingua	victoria
memoria	vita
mensa	

Numbers

unus	sex
duo	septem
tres	octo
quáttuor	novem
quinque	decem
	centum
	mille

Grammar Forms

Verb Personal Endings

-o	-mus
-s	-tis
-t	-nt

1st Conjugation

voco	vocamus
vocas	vocatis
vocat	vocant

Irregular verb *to be*

sum	sumus
es	estis
est	sunt

1st Declension

mensa	mensae
mensae	mensarum
mensae	mensis
mensam	mensas
mensa	mensis

Latin Sayings

Caelum et terra   E pluribus unum
Ora et labora.   Labor omnia vincit.
Mater Italiae — Roma

A. Copy each vocabulary word on a separate sheet of paper and translate.

B. Answer questions in Latin.

1. Give words for four female persons. _____, _____, _____,

_____

2. Give words for three places. _____, _____, _____

3. Name an article of clothing and a piece of furniture. _____

4. Give two words for land. _____, _____

5. Give two verbs for how we feel about God. _____, _____

6. Give two verbs for how we speak to God. _____, _____

C. Translate these similar word pairs.

1. He prays _____   you praise _____

2. life _____   road _____

3. I work _____   I free _____

4. I shout _____   I call _____

5. femina _____   filia _____

D. Conjugate these verbs.

libero   paro

_____ _____   _____ _____

_____ _____   _____ _____

_____ _____   _____ _____

clamo

_____ _____

_____ _____

_____ _____

LESSON VI

Latin Saying

Mea culpa   My fault, I am guilty

Vocabulary

1.	**culpa, culpae**	fault, crime
2.	**María, ae**	Mary
3.	**fuga, ae**	flight
4.	**luna, ae**	moon
5.	**unda, ae**	wave
6.	**Hispánia, ae**	Spain
7.	**silva, ae**	forest
8.	**pugno**	I fight
9.	**júdico**	I judge, consider
10.	**óccupo**	I seize

Grammar Forms

First Declension
Case Endings

	Singular	Plural
Nominative	-a	-ae
Genitive	-ae	-arum
Dative	-ae	-is
Accusative	-am	-as
Ablative	-a	-is

A. Translation

1. Labor omnia vincit. _____

2. Pater noster (p. 73) _____

3. One out of many _____

4. What is your first name? _____

5. Hello, teacher _____

B. Grammar

1. Verbs have _____ endings.

2. Nouns have _____ endings.

C. Add correct personal endings.

1. he works	labora___	5. we fight	pugna___
2. she works	labora___	6. they seize	occupa___
3. they pray	ora___	7. you (pl.) judge	judica___
4. you adore	adora___	8. I sail	navig___

D. Derivatives

1. A person with a Spanish ancestry is said to be _____. **(Hispania)**

2. A _____ flight is one that travels to the moon. **(luna)**

3. We knew the house was _____ because we saw cars in the driveway. **(occupo)**

4. A _____ is one who is fleeing justice. **(fuga)**

5. Harrisburg is the capital of _____. **(silva)**

Advanced Derivatives

6. A bully has a _____ personality. **(pugno)**

7. People who leave their homes because of war or other disasters are _____. **(fuga)**

8. The Bluegrass region of Kentucky has _____ hills. **(unda)**

9. The senators were _____ with phone calls. **(unda)**

10. In a _____ setting there are lots of trees. **(silva)**

LESSON VII

Latin Saying

Anno Domini, A.D.　　　　　　In the year of our Lord

Vocabulary

1.	**stella, ae**	star
2.	**ursa, ae**	bear
3.	**ira, ae**	anger
4.	**servus**	slave
5.	**amícus**	friend
6.	**annus**	year
7.	**fílius**	son
8.	**dóminus**	Lord, master
9.	**ante**	before
10.	**post**	after

Grammar Forms

First Declension

	S.	*Pl.*
Nominative	**terra**	**terrae**
Genitive	**terrae**	**terrárum**
Dative	**terrae**	**terris**
Accusative	**terram**	**terras**
Ablative	**terra**	**terris**

A. Translation

1. Mea culpa   _____
2. Work conquers all.   _____
3. One out of many   _____
4. Quid agis   (p. 74)   _____
5. Satis bene   (p. 74)   _____
6. Surgite   (p. 74)   _____

B. Grammar

1. Latin has no words for the articles_____ and _____.
2. In English _____ words are needed for a sentence, a _____
   and a _____.
3. A verb _____ with its subject in person and number.

C. Translate these Latin sentences.

1. Puella vocat. _____
2. Maria orat. _____
3. Nauta navigat. _____
4. Nauta clamat. _____
5. Servus pugnat. _____

6. Italia occupat. _____
7. Regina orat. _____
8. Gallia superat. _____
9. Femina adorat. _____
10. Filia portat. _____

D. Derivatives

1. The Big Dipper is also called _____ Major. (**ursa**)
2. The Big Dipper is a _____. (**stella**)
3. Christmas is an _____ event. (**annus**)

Advanced Derivatives

4. He could _____ the group because of his forceful personality. (**dominus**)
5. Obedience is a _____ duty. (**filius**)
6. Their parting was strained but _____. (**amicus**)
7. She was _____ when he forgot to call. (**ira**)

LESSON VIII

Latin Saying

Semper fidelis   Always faithful

— motto of the U.S. Marine Corps

Vocabulary

1.	**Deus**	God, god
2.	**Christus**	Christ
3.	**Jesus**	Jesus
4.	**legátus**	lieutenant, envoy
5.	**discípulus**	student
6.	**fama, ae**	fame, rumor
7.	**grátia, ae**	grace
8.	**hora, ae**	hour
9.	**semper**	always
10.	**saepe**	often

Grammar Forms

Second Declension Masculine

	S.	Pl.
Nominative	**servus**	**servi**
Genitive	**servi**	**servórum**
Dative	**servo**	**servis**
Accusative	**servum**	**servos**
Ablative	**servo**	**servis**

A. Translation

1. Anno Domini, A.D. _____

2. My fault _____

3. What is your first name? _____

4. Quid agis? _____

5. Labor omnia vincit. _____

6. Satis bene _____

B. Grammar

1. There are _____ declensions in Latin.

2. First declension nouns end in the letter _____.

3. A declension is a group of nouns that all have the same or similar case _____.

C. Circle plural endings and translate.

1. culpae _____
2. silvae _____
3. undae _____
4. mensae _____
5. lunae _____
6. stellae _____

7. girls _____
8. queens _____
9. hours _____
10. roads _____
11. bears _____
12. women _____

D. Singular subjects. Translate these sentences.

1. Deus amat. _____
2. Dominus judicat. _____
3. Legatus occupat. _____

4. Discipulus laborat. _____
5. Regina ambulat. _____
6. Nauta clamat. _____

E. Derivatives

1. _____ is another word for God. (**Deus**)

2. A _____ is one who follows a teacher. (**discipulus**)

3. Parents must _____ children. (**discipulus**)

4. An attitude of _____ is pleasing to God. (**gratia**)

LESSON IX

Latin Saying

Senatus Populusque Romanus
S.P.Q.R.

The Senate and People of Rome

Vocabulary

1.	**gládius, gladii**	sword
2.	**murus, i**	wall
3.	**ludus, i**	game, school
4.	**pópulus, i**	people
5.	**ánimus, i**	mind, spirit
6.	**pecúnia, ae**	money
7.	**ecclésia, ae**	church
8.	**áquila, ae**	eagle
9.	**coróna, ae**	crown
10.	**mora, ae**	delay

Grammar Forms

2nd Declension
Case Endings - Masculine

	Singular	*Plural*
Nominative	-us	-i
Genitive	-i	-orum
Dative	-o	-is
Accusative	-um	-os
Ablative	-o	-is

A. Translation

1. How are you?   _____
2. Semper fidelis   _____
3. Surgite   _____
4. Pray and work.   _____
5. In the year of Our Lord, A.D.   _____
6. Valete, discipuli   _____

B. Grammar

The _____ case is always used for the subject of a sentence.

C. Circle plural endings and translate.

1. gladii   _____   6. walls   _____
2. servi   _____   7. students _____
3. filii   _____   8. friends   _____
4. legati   _____   9. years   _____
5. ludi   _____   10. crowns   _____

D. Singular and Plural subjects. Translate these sentences.

1. Gladius superat. _____   5. Servus pugnat.   _____
2. Gladii superant. _____   6. Servi pugnant.   _____
3. Legatus portat. _____   7. Puella laudat.   _____
4. Legati portant. _____   8. Puellae laudant. _____

E. Derivatives

1. _____ fought in the Colosseum. (**gladius**)
2. The candidate was _____ with the people. (**populus**)

Advanced Derivatives

3. The _____ of Charlemagne took place on Christmas day in Rome. (**corona**)
4. A _____ on homework would be nice. (**mora**)
5. His _____ comment caused everyone to laugh. (**ludus**)
6. His _____ interests were reflected in his large bank account. (**pecunia**)
7. A wall painting is called a _____ (**murus**)
8. The _____ nose is a characteristic Roman feature. (**aquila**)

LESSON X

Latin Saying

Stupor mundi   Wonder of the world

Vocabulary

1. **mundus, i**   world
2. **sócius, i**   ally
3. **núntius, i**   messenger, message
4. **bárbarus, i**   barbarian
5. **campus, i**   field, plain
6. **capíllus, i**   hair
7. **cibus, i**   food
8. **equus, i**   horse
9. **ventus, i**   wind
10. **locus, i**   place

Grammar Forms

Second Declension

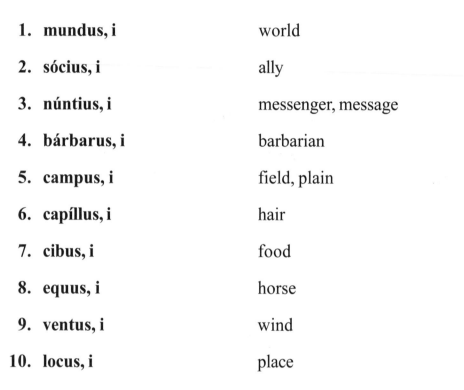

	S.	Pl.
Nominative	campus	campi
Genitive	campi	campórum
Dative	campo	campis
Accusative	campum	campos
Ablative	campo	campis

A. Translation

1. Senatus Populusque Romanus, _____
   S.P.Q.R.

2. Vale, magister _____

3. Surgite _____

4. Always faithful _____

5. Heaven and earth _____

B. Grammar

1. Using NGDAA, write the names of all five cases of nouns.

   _____, _____, _____,

   _____, _____

2. Which case is used for the subject of a sentence? _____

C. Write these singular and plural nouns in Latin.

1. horse _____	4. worlds _____	7. crown _____
2. horses _____	5. Church _____	8. crowns _____
3. world _____	6. churches _____	9. places _____

D. Add personal endings to make the verb agree with the subject.

1. Equus porta_____ .

2. Socii pugna_____ .

3. Barbari pugna_____ .

4. Ecclesiae lauda_____ .

5. Nautae ora_____ .

6. Servus labora_____ .

E. Give the Latin root of these English derivatives.

1. social _____	4. barbaric _____	7. equine _____
2. mundane _____	5. location _____	8. equestrian _____
3. capillary _____	6. announce _____	9. ventilate _____

REVIEW LESSON II

Vocabulary

First Declension Nouns

aquila	ira
corona	luna
culpa	Maria
ecclesia	mora
fama	pecunia
fuga	silva
gratia	stella
Hispania	unda
hora	ursa

Second Declension Nouns

amicus	filius
animus	gladius
annus	legatus
barbarus	locus
campus	ludus
capillus	mundus
Christus	murus
cibus	nuntius
Deus	populus
discipulus	socius
dominus	servus
equus	ventus

First Conjugation Verbs

pugno
judico
occupo

Other words

ante	saepe
post	Jesus
semper	

Grammar Forms

First Declension
Case Endings

-a	-ae
-ae	-arum
-ae	-is
-am	-as
-a	-is

Second Declension - Masculine
Case Endings

-us	-i
-i	-orum
-o	-is
-um	-os
-o	-is

Second Declension

servus	servi
servi	servorum
servo	servis
servum	servos
servo	servis

Latin Sayings

Mea culpa
Anno Domini, A.D.
Semper fidelis

Senatus Populusque Romanus
Stupor mundi

A. Copy vocabulary words and translate.

B. Answer questions in Latin.

1. Give four names for God. _____ , _____ , _____ ,

   _____

2. Name three animals. _____ , _____ , _____

3. Name two things you can see in the heavens. _____ , _____

4. Give two words having to do with education. _____ , _____

5. Give two words having to do with time. _____ , _____

6. Name two types of land regions. _____ , _____

7. Name two things you could find on a person's head. _____ ,

   _____

8. Give two words for 'friend'. _____ , _____

9. Give three words associated with the Roman army. _____ ,

   _____ , _____

10. Name two things Christ rules. _____ , _____

C. Translate these word groups with similar sounds or meanings.

1. annus _____ animus _____ amicus _____
2. filia _____ filius _____
3. mundus _____ murus _____
4. fuga _____ fama _____
5. ursa _____ unda _____
6. gloria _____ fama _____

D. Decline the following nouns.

filius   puella   dominus

_____   _____   _____   _____   _____   _____

_____   _____   _____   _____   _____   _____

_____   _____   _____   _____   _____   _____

_____   _____   _____   _____   _____   _____

_____   _____   _____   _____   _____   _____

LESSON XI

Latin Saying

Ante bellum   Before the war

Vocabulary

1. **bellum, i**   war
2. **donum, i**   gift
3. **óppidum, i**   town
4. **telum, i**   weapon
5. **verbum, i**   word
6. **regnum, i**   kingdom
7. **fruméntum, i**   grain
8. **signum, i**   sign, standard
9. **impérium, i**   command, empire
10. **proélium, i**   battle

Grammar Forms

Second Declension Neuter

	S.	Pl.
Nom.	donum	dona
Gen.	doni	donórum
Dat.	dono	donis
Acc.	donum	dona
Abl.	dono	donis

A. Respond to the following in Latin.

1. Quid est tuum praenomen? _____

2. Quid agis? _____

3. Salvete, discipuli. _____

4. Vale, magister. _____

B. Grammar

1. All nouns whose genitive singular ends in *ae* belong to the _____ declension.

2. All nouns whose genitive singular ends in *i* belong to the _____ declension.

3. The second declension has two groups of nouns. In the nominative case, some end in _____ and others end in _____.

C. Translate these sentences.

1. Portas. _____

2. Nuntius vocat. _____

3. Equi laborant. _____

4. Socii pugnant. _____

5. Barbari clamant. _____

6. Regina liberat. _____

7. Judicamus. _____

8. Paratis. _____

9. Animus superat. _____

10. Populus occupat. _____

11. Ecclesiae orant. _____

12. Maria ambulat. _____

D. Derivatives

1. He gave a large _____ to the church. (**dona**)

2. An _____ modifies a verb. (**verbum**)

3. He gave a _____ to start the race. (**signum**)

4. During the _____ of Queen Elizabeth, England was at peace. (**regnum**)

5. Her _____ was required to seal the contract. (**signum**)

6. At one time the sun never set on the British _____. (**imperium**)

Advanced Derivatives

7. Her arrogance showed in her _____ manner. (**imperium**)

8. His _____ actions almost caused a war. (**bellum**)

LESSON XII

Latin Saying

Excelsior!   Ever higher!

Vocabulary

1. **gáudium, i**   joy, gladness

2. **auxílium, i**   help, aid

3. **débitum, i**   debt, trespass

4. **caelum, i**   heaven

5. **peccátum, i**   mistake, sin

6. **vallum, i**   wall, rampart

7. **praémium, i**   reward

8. **vinum, i**   wine

9. **tergum, i**   back

10. **forum, i**   forum

Grammar Forms

Second Declension Neuter
Case Endings

	S.	*Pl.*
Nom.	-um	-a
Gen.	-i	-orum
Dat.	-o	-is
Acc.	-um	-a
Abl.	-o	-is

A. Translation

1. Ante bellum _____
2. The Senate and People of Rome _____
3. Stupor mundi _____

B. Grammar

1. What are the three genders of nouns? _____, _____, _____
2. Second declension nouns that end in *us* are _____ in gender.
3. Second declension nons that end in *um* are _____ in gender.
4. Decline the following words:

oppidum   telum

_____ _____   _____ _____

_____ _____   _____ _____

_____ _____   _____ _____

_____ _____   _____ _____

_____ _____   _____ _____

C. Circle Latin case endings and translate.

1. oppidum _____   5. verbum _____   9. sins _____
2. oppida _____   6. verba _____   10. sin _____
3. dona _____   7. rampart _____   11. joy _____
4. donum _____   8. ramparts _____   12. joys _____

D. Translation

1. Oppidum orat. _____   5. Caelum vocat. _____
2. Oppida pugnant. _____   6. Auxilium superat. _____
3. Verbum laudat. _____   7. Regnum superat. _____
4. Verba laudant. _____   8. Oppida laborant. _____

E. Derivatives

1. He owed the man a _____ he could never repay. (**debitum**)
2. She wore a _____ dress to the ladies' tea. (**gaudium**)
3. Public issues can be discussed at a town _____. (**forum**)
   Advanced Derivatives
4. Cherubim are _____ creatures. (**caelum**)
5. The Romans used _____ troops from other nations. (**auxilium**)
6. The opposite of a credit is a _____. (**debitum**)

LESSON XIII

Latin Saying

Sanctus, Sanctus, Sanctus,   Holy, Holy, Holy
Dominus Deus Sabaoth   Lord God of Hosts

Vocabulary

1. **altus, alta, altum**   high, deep
2. **bonus, a, um**   good
3. **longus, a, um**   long
4. **malus, a, um**   bad
5. **multus, a, um**   much, many
6. **magnus, a, um**   large, great
7. **plenus, a, um**   full
8. **sanctus, a, um**   holy, saint
9. **tutus, a, um**   safe
10. **parvus, a, um**   small

Grammar Forms

First and Second Declension Adjectives - Singular

	M.	*F.*	*N.*
Nom.	bonus	bona	bonum
Gen.	boni	bonae	boni
Dat.	bono	bonae	bono
Acc.	bonum	bonam	bonum
Abl.	bono	bona	bono

A. Translation

1. Gratias tibi ago _____

2. Surgite _____

3. Oremus _____

4. Excelsior! _____

5. Ante bellum _____

6. Sanctus, Sanctus, Sanctus,
   Dominus Deus Sabaoth _____

B. Grammar

1. An adjective is a word that _____ a noun or pronoun.

2. Adjectives can change their _____ to agree with nouns they modify.

C. Translate.

1. parvum debitum _____

2. frumentum plenum _____

3. vita bona _____

4. memoria mala _____

5. patria tuta _____

6. magnus amicus _____

7. altum vallum _____

8. multus cibus _____

9. parvum gaudium _____

10. legatus malus _____

11. Deus bonus _____

12. Sanctus Deus _____

D. Derivatives

1. Grapes are _____ this year. (**plenus**)

2. To _____ means to make holy. (**sanctus**)

3. _____ lines run north and south. (**longus**)

4. The _____ followed Christ. (**multus**)

5. It is harder to breathe at high _____. (**altus**)

6. To _____ means to make large. (**magnus**)

Advanced Derivatives

7. His _____ showed in his hateful words. (**malus**)

8. His grades weren't just bad, they were _____. (**malus**)

LESSON XIV

Latin Saying

Novus ordo seclorum New order of the ages

Vocabulary

1. **aetérnus, a, um** eternal, everlasting
2. **certus, a, um** certain, sure
3. **primus, a, um** first
4. **secúndus, a, um** second
5. **tértius, a, um** third
6. **próximus, a, um** nearest, next
7. **summus, a, um** highest, greatest
8. **totus, a, um** whole
9. **solus, a, um** alone, only
10. **novus, a, um** new

Grammar Forms

First and Second Declension
Adjectives - Plural

	M.	F.	N.
Nom.	boni	bonae	bona
Gen.	bonórum	bonárum	bonórum
Dat.	bonis	bonis	bonis
Acc.	bonos	bonas	bona
Abl.	bonis	bonis	bonis

A. Translation

1. Oremus   _____

2. Surgite   _____

3. Ever higher!   _____

4. Sanctus, Sanctus Sanctus,   _____
   Dominus Deus Sabaoth   _____

5. Stupor mundi   _____

B. Grammar

1. Adjectives and the nouns they modify must agree in _____ ,
   _____ and _____ .

2. In Latin, adjectives can be written _____ or _____ .
   the noun.

C. Translate.

1. Stellae sunt magnae. _____
2. Via est nova. _____
3. Filius est primus. _____
4. Legati sunt mali. _____
5. Deus est sanctus. _____
6. Oppida sunt tuta. _____
7. Murus est proximus. _____
8. Luna est plena. _____
9. Roma est aeterna. _____
10. Peccata sunt mala. _____
11. Vallum est summum. _____
12. Frumentum est plenum. _____

D. Derivatives

1. Lindbergh flew _____ across the Atlantic. (**solus**)

2. He walked to the _____ of the hill. (**summus**)

3. An _____ answer is close, but not exact. (**proximus**)

Advanced Derivatives

4. He was a _____ at golf. (**novus**)

5. Jesus sought _____ when the crowd became large. (**solus**)

6. It wasn't his primary or secondary objective, but only _____ . (**tertius**)

LESSON XV

Latin Saying

Nunc aut numquam   Now or never

Vocabulary

1.	**nunc**	now
2.	**clam**	secretly
3.	**non**	not
4.	**bene**	well
5.	**inter**	between
6.	**numquam**	never
7.	**contra**	against
8.	**sub**	under
9.	**supra**	above
10.	**ex**	out of

Grammar Forms

Irregular verb *to be able*

	S.	Pl.
1st Per.	**possum**	**póssumus**
2nd Per.	**potes**	**potéstis**
3rd. Per.	**potest**	**possunt**

A. Translation

1. Holy, Holy, Holy, Lord God of Hosts _____

   _____

2. Novus ordo seclorum _____

3. Ever higher! _____

4. Before the war _____

5. Gratias tibi ago _____

B. Grammar

1. An adverb is a word that modifies a _____.

2. An adjective is a word that modifies a _____ or _____.

C. Translate.

1. possum _____
2. est _____
3. potest _____
4. possumus _____
5. sunt _____
6. Laborant. _____
7. magna ursa _____
8. multus cibus _____

9. Stella est parva. _____
10. Servus est solus. _____
11. Gaudium est magnum. _____
12. Puella orat. _____
13. Femina portat. _____
14. Legati pugnant. _____
15. Nautae navigant. _____
16. Puellae orant. _____

D. Derivatives

1. The movie was so long that it had an _____. (**inter**)

2. The students went out the _____. (**ex**)

3. The student _____ his teacher. (**contra**)

4. A _____ is an underground train. (**sub**)

Advanced Derivatives

5. The _____ meeting was observed by spies. (**clam**)

Vocabulary

Second Declension Nouns
Neuter

auxilium	peccatum
bellum	praemium
caelum	proelium
debitum	regnum
donum	signum
forum	telum
frumentum	tergum
gaudium	vallum
imperium	verbum
oppidum	vinum

Adjectives

aeternus	plenus
altus	primus
bonus	proximus
certus	sanctus
longus	secundus
magnus	solus
malus	summus
multus	tertius
novus	totus
parvus	tutus

Other words

bene	clam	contra	ex	inter
non	numquam	nunc	sub	supra

Grammar Forms

2nd Declension Nouns

Neuter	
-um	-a
-i	-orum
-o	-is
-um	-a
-o	-is
donum	dona
doni	donorum
dono	donis
donum	dona
dono	donis

Adjectives

Singular		
bonus	bona	bonum
boni	bonae	boni
bono	bonae	bono
bonum	bonam	bonum
bono	bona	bono

Plural		
boni	bonae	bona
bonorum	bonarum	bonorum
bonis	bonis	bonis
bonos	bonas	bona
bonis	bonis	bonis

Irregular verb *possum*

possum	possumus
potes	potestis
potest	possunt

Latin Sayings

Ante bellum
Excelsior!
Sanctus, Sanctus, Sanctus,
       Dominus Deus Sabaoth.
Novus ordo seclorum
Nunc aut numquam

EXERCISES *for Review Lesson 3*

A. Copy vocabulary words and translate.

B. Answer questions in Latin.

1. Give two words for sin. _____, _____
2. Name two substances used in Holy Communion. _____,

   _____

3. Give two words for government power. _____,

   _____

4. Name two things carried in battle. _____, _____
5. Give six adjectives that describe God. _____, _____,

   _____, _____, _____, _____

C. Translate these word pairs.

murus	_____	vallum	_____
proelium	_____	praemium	_____
summus	_____	sumus	_____
tutus	_____	totus	_____

D. Decline these nouns on a separate sheet of paper.

peccatum   debitum

E. Decline these adjectives in all three genders on a separate sheet of paper.

sanctus   malus

LESSON XVI

Latin Saying

Veni, vidi, vici.
    —Julius Caesar

I came, I saw, I conquered.

Vocabulary

1.	**móneo**	I warn
2.	**vídeo**	I see
3.	**térreo**	I frighten
4.	**hábeo**	I have
5.	**móveo**	I move
6.	**tímeo**	I fear
7.	**dóceo**	I teach
8.	**débeo**	I owe, ought
9.	**prohíbeo**	I prevent
10.	**júbeo**	I order, command

Grammar Forms

Second Conjugation

	S.	Pl.
1st P.	**móneo**	**monémus**
2nd P.	**mones**	**monétis**
3rd P.	**monet**	**monent**

A. Translation

1. Nunc aut numquam _____
2. Novus ordo seclorum _____
3. Excelsior! _____
4. Wonder of the world _____
5. Thank you _____
6. Stand up _____
7. Oremus _____
8. Vale, magister. _____

B. Grammar

1. In the second conjugation the stem vowel is the letter _____.
2. In the first conjugation the stem vowel is the letter _____.
3. Conjugate *video* and translate.

_____ _____   _____ _____

_____ _____   _____ _____

_____ _____   _____ _____

C. Circle personal endings and translate.

1. vident _____   9. Legati vident. _____
2. Puella videt. _____   10. Deus monet. _____
3. monet _____   11. debeo _____
4. Amicus monet. _____   12. debes _____
5. monemus _____   13. debetis _____
6. mones _____   14. movet _____
7. videmus _____   15. movetis _____
8. video _____

D. Derivatives

1. The mistake was so clear it should have been self-_____. (**video**)
2. The signs made it clear that hunting was strictly _____. (**prohibeo**)
3. His _____ approach to the subject showed he didn't know very much about it. (**timeo**)
   Advanced Derivatives
4. The study hall _____ went to sleep. (**moneo**)
5. He tried to _____ his tennis opponent by bragging. (**timeo**)

LESSON XVII

Latin Saying

Agnus Dei, qui tollis peccata mundi.

Lamb of God who takes away the sins of the world.

Vocabulary

1.	**agnus, i**	lamb
2.	**ínsula, ae**	island
3.	**óculus, i**	eye
4.	**appéllo**	I speak to, address
5.	**narro**	I tell
6.	**do**	I give
7.	**meus, a, um**	my
8.	**tuus, a, um**	your (to one person)
9.	**injúria, ae**	injury
10.	**sédeo**	I sit

Grammar Forms

Second Conjugation

	S.	Pl.
1st P.	**habeo**	**habémus**
2nd P.	**habes**	**habétis**
3rd P.	**habet**	**habent**

EXERCISES *for Lesson 17*

A. Translation

1. St. Benedict's Rule _____
2. Now or never _____
3. Pre-civil war south _____
4. Motto of the Marine Corps _____

B. Grammar

1. Conjugate (a) do and (b) sedeo on a separate sheet of paper.
2. Decline (a) oculus and (b) peccatum on a separate sheet of paper.

C. Translate these nouns and adjectives.

1. multae puellae _____
2. puellae bonae _____
3. primus filius _____
4. peccata mala _____
5. oculus tuus _____
6. agnus meus _____
7. aeterna vita _____
8. multi barbari _____

D. Translate these sentences.

1. Sum puella. _____
2. Bonus es. _____
3. Parant. _____
4. Movet. _____
5. Terremus. _____
6. Jubetis. _____
7. Regina est bona. _____
8. Regina videt. _____
9. Amici docent. _____
10. Christus jubet. _____
11. Nuntii prohibent. _____
12. Jesus docet. _____

E. Derivatives

1. He could see the bird through his _____. (**oculus**)
2. The _____ of the story had a beautiful voice. (**narro**)

Advanced Derivatives

3. He led the _____ life of a hermit. (**insula**)
4. _____ rock is formed from layers of sediment. (**sedeo**)

LESSON XVIII

Latin Saying

Rident stolidi verba Latina.
   —Ovid

Fools laugh at the Latin language.

Vocabulary

1.	**hábito**	I live, dwell
2.	**cena, ae**	dinner
3.	**auróra, ae**	dawn
4.	**auríga, ae**	charioteer
5.	**lavo**	I wash
6.	**sicut**	as
7.	**pugna, ae**	fight
8.	**fenéstra, ae**	window
9.	**hortus, i**	garden
10.	**nimbus, i**	cloud

Grammar Forms

Future Tense Endings

	S.	*Pl.*
1st P.	**bo**	**bimus**
2nd P.	**bis**	**bitis**
3rd P.	**bit**	**bunt**

A. Translation

1. Agnus Dei, qui tollis peccata mundi. _____

_____

2. I came, I saw, I conquered. _____
3. The Senate and People of Rome _____

B. Grammar

1. The subject and verb must agree in _____ and _____.
2. Do verbs have gender? _____.

C. Translate these verbs from Lessons 16 and 17.

1. habemus _____
2. narras _____
3. dat _____
4. sedent _____
5. dant _____
6. sedemus _____

7. narrant _____
8. habet _____
9. jubes _____
10. jubetis _____
11. timemus _____
12. docent _____

D. Translate these words from today's lesson.

1. habitas _____
2. habitamus _____
3. lavat _____
4. lavant _____

5. hortus meus _____
6. fenestrae _____
7. multi nimbi _____
8. cena tua _____

E. Derivatives

1. _____ flows out of active volcanoes. (**lava**)
2. The _____ borealis is also called the Northern Lights. (**aurora**)

Advanced Derivatives

3. A _____ is a sink for washing hands. (**lavo**)
4. He has a _____ personality and is always ready for a fight. (**pugna**)
5. The house was not a fit _____. (**habito**)
6. _____ is the study of gardening. (**hortus**)

LESSON XIX

Latin Saying

Quo vadis?   Where are you going?

Vocabulary

1.	**virgo**	maiden, virgin
2.	**libra, ae**	pair of scales
3.	**scórpio**	scorpion
4.	**sagittárius, i**	archer
5.	**cápricorn**	goat
6.	**aquárius, i**	water carrier
7.	**pisces**	fish
8.	**áries**	ram
9.	**taurus, i**	bull
10.	**géminus, i**	twin
11.	**cancer**	crab
12.	**leo**	lion

Grammar Forms

First Conjugation Future Tense

	S.	Pl.
1st P.	**vocabo**	**vocabimus**
2nd P.	**vocabis**	**vocabitis**
3rd P.	**vocabit**	**vocabunt**

A. Translation

1. Rident stolidi verba Latina. _____
2. Thank you _____
3. Motto on our coin money _____
4. I came, I saw, I conquered. _____

B. Grammar

1. There are _____ tenses in Latin and English.
2. In English the future tense is formed by adding the helping verb _____.
3. Conjugate in the future tense and translate on a separate sheet of paper.

   (a) specto   (b) paro

C. Circle the future endings and translate these verbs from Lesson 1.

1. amabit _____
2. amabo _____
3. portabunt _____
4. portabimus _____
5. laudabitis _____
6. orabis _____
7. orabit _____
8. laborabit _____
9. laborabo _____
10. laborabis _____
11. amabitis _____
12. orabunt _____
13. portabo _____
14. laudabimus _____
15. laudabis _____

D. Translate these sentences.

1. Vallum est altum. _____
2. Vinum est novum. _____
3. Debita sunt mala. _____
4. Gaudium est magnum. _____
5. Praemium est primum. _____
6. Maria sedet. _____
7. Amici narrant. _____
8. Puellae dant. _____
9. Barbari habitant. _____
10. Filii docent. _____

LESSON XX

Latin Saying

Alma mater   Nurturing mother

Vocabulary

1. **frater, fratris**   brother
2. **pater, patris**   father
3. **mater, matris**   mother
4. **lex, legis**   law
5. **rex, regis**   king
6. **pecúnia, ae**   money
7. **mensa, ae**   table
8. **lingua, ae**   language
9. **próximus, a, um**   nearest, next
10. **et**   and

Grammar Forms

Second Conjugation Future Tense

	S.	Pl.
1st P.	**monébo**	**monébimus**
2nd P.	**monébis**	**monébitis**
3rd P.	**monébit**	**monébunt**

A. Translation

1. Quo vadis?   _____
2. Motto on eagle side of The Great Seal   _____
3. Repete   _____
4. Repetite   _____

B. Grammar

1. Nouns whose genitive singular ends in _____ belong to the third declension.
2. The nominative singular of third declension nouns is_____.
3. There are _____ declensions in Latin.

C. Circle the future endings and translate these verbs from Lesson 16.

1. videbo   _____   9. timebis   _____
2. prohibebimus   _____   10. terrebimus   _____
3. habebit   _____   11. jubebo   _____
4. habebunt   _____   12. jubebunt   _____
5. movebis   _____   13. debebitis   _____
6. movebitis   _____   14. debebit   _____
7. docebo   _____   15. monebimus   _____
8. docebunt   _____

D. Circle the present endings and translate.

1. vides   _____   9. movetis   _____
2. videt   _____   10. sedent   _____
3. terremus   _____   11. jubetis   _____
4. timetis   _____   12. jubet   _____
5. monent   _____   13. sedemus   _____
6. docemus   _____   14. habes   _____
7. debes   _____   15. habet   _____
8. debet   _____

E. Derivatives

1. A _____ is a social club for men. (**frater**)
2. Holy _____ is ordained by God. (**mater**)
3. The king of the dinosaurs was _____. (**rex**)
4. The _____ passes laws. (**lex, legis**)

~ 53 ~

Vocabulary

Second conjugation verbs

debeo	prohibeo
doceo	sedeo
habeo	terreo
jubeo	timeo
moneo	video
moveo	

First conjugation verbs

appello
do
habito
lavo
narro

1st declension nouns

auriga
aurora
cena
fenestra
injuria
insula
pugna

2nd declension masculine nouns

agnus
hortus
oculus
nimbus

3rd declension nouns

frater, fratris
lex, legis
mater, matris
pater, patris
rex, regis

Constellation names

virgo	pisces
libra	aries
scorpio	taurus
sagittarius	geminus
capricorn	cancer
aquarius	leo

Adjectives

meus
tuus

Other words

et
sicut

Grammar Forms

Future Tense Endings

bo	bimus
bis	bitis
bit	bunt

First Conjugation Future

vocabo	vocabimus
vocabis	vocabitis
vocabit	vocabunt

Second Conjugation Present		Second Conjugation Future	
moneo	monemus	monebo	monebimus
mones	monetis	monebis	monebitis
monet	monent	monebit	monebunt

Latin Sayings

Veni, vidi, vici.

Agnus Dei, qui tollis peccata mundi.

Rident stolidi verba Latina.

Quo vadis?

Alma mater

EXERCISES *for Review Lesson 4*

A. Copy vocabulary words and translate.

B. Answer questions in Latin.

1. Name three members of a family. _____, _____, _____
2. Name three things Jesus is. _____, _____, _____
3. Name the constellations that are animals.

_____   _____   _____

_____   _____   _____

_____

4. Name the constellations that are people.

_____   _____   _____

_____

C. Translate these similar word pairs.

habeo	_____	habito	_____
jubeo	_____	judico	_____
moveo	_____	moneo	_____
terreo	_____	timeo	_____
appello	_____	voco	_____
auriga	_____	aurora	_____
pugno	_____	pugna	_____
debeo	_____	doceo	_____
insula	_____	injuria	_____

LESSON XXI

Latin Saying

Pax Romana   The Roman Peace

Vocabulary

1. **lux, lucis**   light
2. **véritas, veritátis**   truth
3. **Caesar, Caésaris**   Caesar
4. **pons, pontis**   bridge
5. **pax, pacis**   peace
6. **caput, cápitis**   head
7. **hostis, hostis**   enemy
8. **ordo, órdinis**   rank
9. **tempus, témporis**   time
10. **ignis, ignis**   fire

Grammar Forms

Imperfect Tense Endings

	S.	*Pl.*
1st P.	**bam**	**bamus**
2nd P.	**bas**	**batis**
3rd P.	**bat**	**bant**

A. Translation

1. Symbol of the Roman Republic   _____
2. Fools laugh at the Latin language.   _____
3. Where are you going?   _____

B. Grammar

In Latin there are _____ conjugations and _____ tenses.

C. Translate these nouns into Latin in both the singular and plural nominative. They can be found in Lessons 17 & 18.

1. fight   _____ _____
2. garden   _____ _____
3. cloud   _____ _____
4. dawn   _____ _____
5. charioteer   _____ _____

6. dinner   _____ _____
7. lamb   _____ _____
8. eye   _____ _____
9. injury   _____ _____
10. island   _____ _____

D. Circle endings and translate.

1. lavo   _____
2. appellant   _____
3. narrat   _____
4. damus   _____
5. habitatis   _____
6. das   _____

7. lavabit   _____
8. appellabimus   _____
9. narrabis   _____
10. dabo   _____
11. habitabunt   _____
12. habitabitis   _____

E. Derivatives

1. The most sacred building in Rome was the Temple of Jupiter, or the
_____. (**caput**)
2. _____ rock comes from volcanoes. (**ignis**)
3. _____ is a common name for Satan. (**lux**)
4. The car's _____ wouldn't start. (**ignis**)
5. Austin is the _____ of Texas. (**caput**)
6. When the baby cries, we just give him a _____. (**pax**)
7. We couldn't get a permanent replacement, so we settled for a
_____ one. (**tempus**)

LESSON XXII

Latin Saying

Miles Christi sum.   I am a soldier of Christ.

Vocabulary

1.	**miles, mílitis**	soldier
2.	**mons, montis**	mountain
3.	**canis, canis**	dog
4.	**corpus, córporis**	body
5.	**nomen, nóminis**	name
6.	**fama, ae**	rumor, report
7.	**soror, soróris**	sister
8.	**hora, ae**	hour
9.	**centúrio, centuriónis**	centurion
10.	**cívitas, civitátis**	state

Grammar Forms

First Conjugation Imperfect Tense

	S.	Pl.
1st P.	**vocabam**	**vocabamus**
2nd P.	**vocabas**	**vocabatis**
3rd P.	**vocabat**	**vocabant**

A. Translation

1. Pax Romana _____
2. Nurturing mother _____
3. Repeat (pl.) _____
4. Repeat (s.) _____

B. Grammar

1. Name the three tenses you have learned in Latin. _____,

_____, _____

2. The _____ tense describes an action that is occurring in the past.

C. Circle the imperfect tense endings and translate.

1. laudabam _____
2. amabat _____
3. orabamus _____
4. laborabant _____
5. portabas _____
6. clamabatis _____
7. vocabamus _____
8. superabas _____
9. navigabat _____
10. parabant _____
11. spectabam _____
12. ambulabatis _____
13. adorabat _____
14. liberabas _____
15. occupabamus _____

D. Give the genitive for these 3rd declension nouns from lessons 20, 21.

1. lux _____
2. pons _____
3. mater _____
4. pater _____
5. rex _____
6. lex _____
7. veritas _____
8. Caesar _____
9. pax _____
10. frater _____
11. caput _____
12. ordo _____
13. tempus _____
14. ignis _____
15. hostis _____

E. Derivatives

1. A _____ is a social club for women. (**soror**)
2. Western _____ has its roots in Rome. (**civitas**)
3. _____ punishment is physical. (**corpus**)
4. Wolves and coyotes are in the _____ family. (**canis**)

LESSON XXIII

Latin Saying

Vox populi, vox dei
—Roman proverb

The voice of the people is the voice of god.

Vocabulary

1. **urbs, urbis**   city
2. **vox, vocis**   voice
3. **légio, legiónis**   legion
4. **homo, hóminis**   man
5. **imperátor, imperatóris**   commander
6. **auríga, ae**   charioteer
7. **ira, ae**   anger
8. **sicut**   as
9. **totus, a, um**   whole
10. **silva, ae**   forest

Grammar Forms

Second Conjugation Imperfect Tense

	S.	*Pl.*
1st P.	**monebam**	**monebamus**
2nd P.	**monebas**	**monebatis**
3rd P.	**monebat**	**monebant**

A. Translation

1. Miles Christi sum. _____

2. The Roman peace _____

3. School one graduated from _____

4. What John the Baptist declared Jesus to be. _____

_____

B. Grammar

1. A noun is a word for a _____, _____ or _____.

2. A verb is a word that shows _____ or _____.

3. An adjective _____ a noun or a pronoun.

C. Supply the correct ending.

1. I was walking   ambula_____

2. He was praying   ora_____

3. She was working   labora_____

4. They were sailing   naviga_____

5. We were praising   lauda_____

6. You(s.) were carrying porta_____

7. He was looking at   specta_____

8. She was warning   mone_____

9. We were moving   move_____

10. They were teaching   doce_____

D. Derivatives

1. The _____ are communities that lie outside the city. (**urbs**)

2. Killing another human being is called _____. (**homo**)

Advanced Derivatives

3. It is hard for mothers not to become _____ at their children when they are not good. (**ira**)

4. _____ means "across the woods." (**silva**)

5. An _____ sentence gives a command. (**imperium**)

LESSON XXIV

Latin Saying

Signum crucis   Sign of the cross

Vocabulary

1. **virtus, virtútis**   courage, virtue
2. **collis, collis**   hill
3. **navis, navis**   ship
4. **nox, noctis**   night
5. **crux, crucis**   cross
6. **tutus, a, um**   safe
7. **praémium, i**   reward
8. **proélium, i**   battle
9. **pátria, ae**   fatherland, country
10. **núntius, i**   messenger, message

Grammar Forms

Declension of First Person Pronouns

S.	*Pl.*
ego	nos
mei	nostri, nostrum
mihi	nobis
me	nos
me	nobis

A. Translation

1. Vox populi, vox dei   _____
2. Confession of sin before worship   _____
3. Dispatch of Julius Caesar   _____
4. I am a soldier of Christ.   _____

B. Give the genitive for these 3rd declension nouns from Lessons 22-24.

1. civitas _____
2. centurio _____
3. miles _____
4. mons _____
5. imperator _____
6. vox _____
7. legio _____
8. homo _____
9. urbs _____
10. canis _____
11. corpus _____
12. soror _____
13. nomen _____
14. nox _____
15. collis _____

C. Translate these imperfect and future verbs into English. Circle the tense endings.

1. monebamus _____
2. monebimus _____
3. timebunt _____
4. timebant _____
5. debebas _____
6. docebat _____
7. docebit _____
8. videbatis _____
9. jubebo _____
10. jubebam _____
11. movebas _____
12. movebis _____
13. terrebamus _____
14. terrebimus _____
15. habebo _____

D. Translate these lines from the Lord's Prayer.

1. Da nobis hodie _____
2. Et ne nos inducas _____
3. Et dimitte nobis _____
4. Sed libera nos a malo _____

E. Derivatives

1. Animals that sleep during the day and are up at night are _____. (**nox**)
2. When the Romans were _____, they were great. (**virtus**)
3. _____ is its own reward. (**virtus**)
4. It was _____ to the crowd that the President would be arriving at any moment. (**nuntio**)

LESSON XXV

Latin Saying

Et tu, Brute?   You too, Brutus?

Vocabulary

1.	**dolor, dolóris**	pain, sorrow
2.	**gens, gentis**	tribe
3.	**pars, partis**	part
4.	**flumen, flúminis**	river
5.	**mors, mortis**	death
6.	**lavo**	I wash
7.	**appéllo**	I call, address
8.	**hábito**	I live
9.	**narro**	I tell
10.	**do**	I give

Grammar Forms

Declension of Second Person Pronouns

S.	*Pl.*
tu	**vos**
tui	**vestri, vestrum**
tibi	**vobis**
te	**vos**
te	**vobis**

A. Translation

1. Caesar's last words _____

2. Signum Crucis _____

3. The voice of the people is the voice of god. _____

_____

B. Translate these sentences.

1. Puellae ambulant. _____
2. Miles monet. _____
3. Navis navigat. _____
4. Mater lavat. _____
5. Rex sedet. _____

6. Pater dat. _____
7. Gens habitat. _____
8. Frater appellat. _____
9. Centurio portat. _____
10. Soror docet. _____

C. Translate these sentences in the imperfect and future tenses.

1. Pons movebit. _____
2. Caesar jubebit. _____
3. Canis terrebat. _____
4. Rex sedebat. _____
5. Imperator videbit. _____

6. Vox laudabit. _____
7. Parabamus. _____
8. Hostis pugnabat. _____
9. Urbs superabit. _____
10. Appellabitis. _____

D. Translate.

1. Regina est bona. _____
2. Roma est aeterna. _____
3. Memoria est mala. _____
4. Aqua est alta. _____
5. Discipuli sunt parvi. _____

6. Domini sunt magni. _____
7. Oppidum est novum. _____
8. Bella sunt mala. _____
9. Gaudium est magnum. _____
10. Debita sunt magna. _____

E. Derivatives

1. A _____ of bread was all there was left to eat. (**pars**).

2. All men are _____. (**mors**)

3. The Way of Sorrows is the _____. (**via**)

4. She is _____ in French and Spanish. (**flumen**)

5. The _____ case is for the possessive. (**gens**)

6. Latin is not dead, it is _____! (**mors**)

Vocabulary

Third declension nouns

Caesar, Caesaris
canis, canis
caput, capitis
centurio, centurionis
civitas, civitatis
collis, collis
corpus, corporis
crux, crucis
dolor, doloris
flumen, fluminis
gens, gentis

homo, hominis
hostis, hostis
ignis, ignis
imperator, imperatoris
legio, legionis
lux, lucis
miles, militis
mons, montis
mors, mortis
navis, navis
nomen, nominis

nox, noctis
ordo, ordinis
pars, partis
pax, pacis
pons, pontis
soror, sororis
tempus, temporis
urbs, urbis
veritas, veritatis
virtus, virtutis
vox, vocis

Review words

appello
auriga, ae
do
fama, ae
habito
hora, ae
ira, ae
lavo
narro

nuntius, i
patria, ae
praemium, i
proelium, i
sicut
silva, ae
totus, a, um
tutus, a, um

Latin Sayings

Pax Romana
Miles Christi Sum.
Vox populi, vox dei
Signum crucis
Et tu, Brute?

Grammar Forms

Pronouns - First Person

S.	Pl.
ego	nos
mei	nostri, nostrum
mihi	nobis
me	nos
me	nobis

Pronouns - Second Person

S.	Pl.
tu	vos
tui	vestri, vestrum
tibi	vobis
te	vos
te	vobis

Imperfect Tense

First Conjugation		Second Conjugation		tense endings	
S.	*Pl.*	*S.*	*Pl.*	*S.*	*Pl.*
vocabam	vocabamus	monebam	monebamus	bam	bamus
vocabas	vocabatis	monebas	monebatis	bas	batis
vocabat	vocabant	monebat	monebant	bat	bant

EXERCISES *for Review Lesson 5*

Give meanings for all words in Review Lesson V.

A. Answer questions in Latin.

1. Give five words having to do with the Roman army. _____,

_____, _____, _____, _____

2. Give four words for geography terms. _____, _____,

_____, _____

3. Give four words associated with Christ and his death. _____,

_____, _____, _____

4. Give three words for what Christ said he is. _____,

_____, _____

B. Give meanings for these groups of similar words.

veritas _____ virtus _____

mons _____ mors _____ mora _____

totus _____ tutus _____ tuus _____

lex _____ lux _____

C. Conjugate these verbs in the present, future, and imperfect tenses on a separate sheet of paper.

     narro   do   sedeo

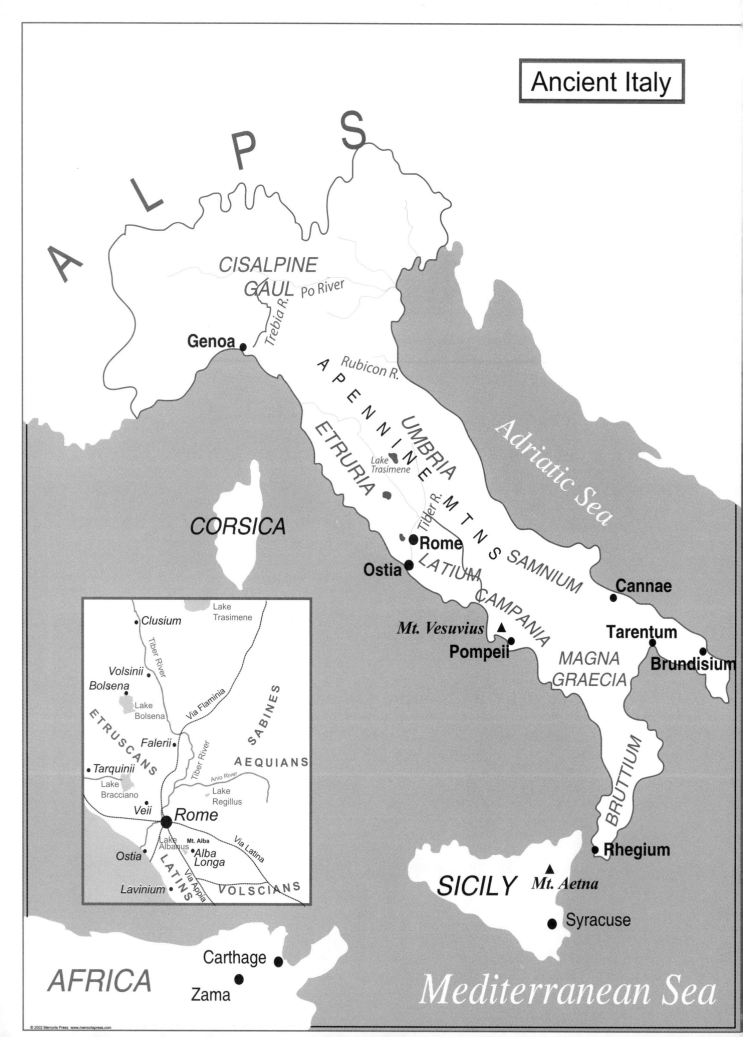

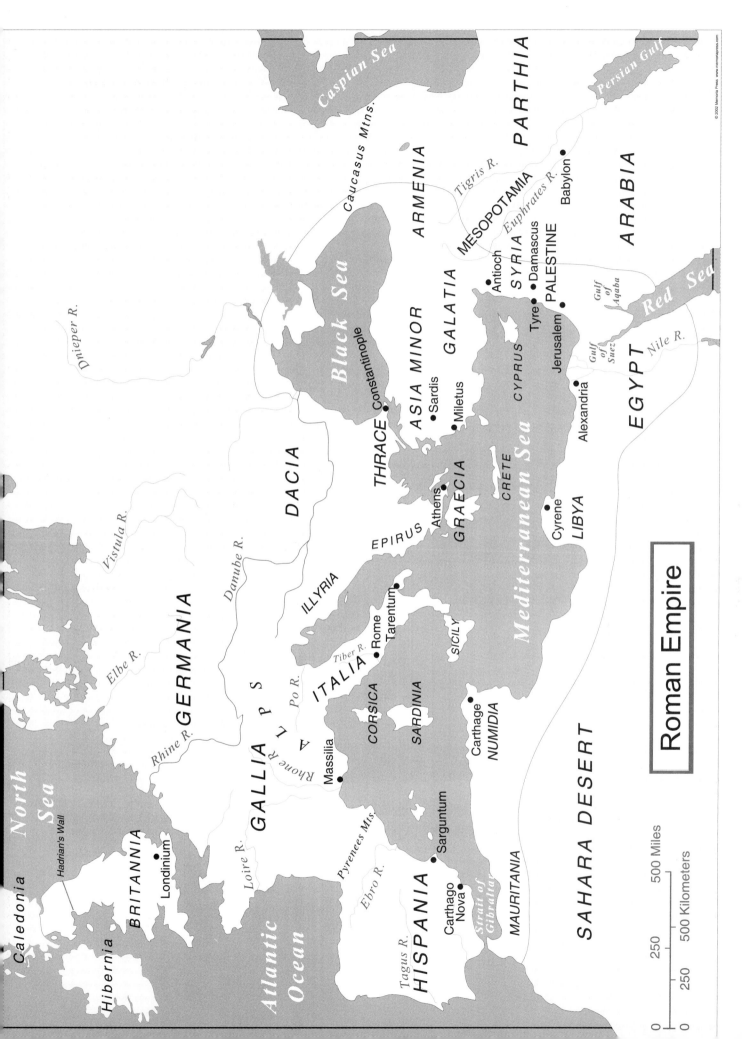

Roman Empire

500 Miles

500 Kilometers

0   250   500

0   250   500

HISTORY QUESTIONS

A COMPREHENSIVE, 30 LESSON FAMOUS MEN OF ROME GUIDE IS ALSO AVAILABLE FROM MEMORIA PRESS.

CHAPTER I

1. In what year was Rome founded?
2. Name the twins who founded Rome.
3. How were the twins saved from drowning?
4. Who nursed the twins as infants?
5. Rome is on what river?
6. How did Romulus and Remus avenge their mother's death?
7. On what hill did Romulus and Remus decide to build their new city?
8. What disagreement did the twins have over the founding of their new city?
9. How did the twins seek a sign from the gods?
10. What did Romulus do to attract people to come and live in Rome?
11. What is the name of the warrior tribe that lived on the mountains near Rome?
12. What is the name of the story which tells how the Romans found their first wives?
13. What is the name for the common people of Rome?
14. What is the name for the noble class of Rome?
15. What is the name of the council of old men who helped rule Rome?
16. According to legend, after Romulus died he appeared to a citizen and said, "Go tell my people that it is the will of the gods that Rome will be _____?

CHAPTER II

17. Who was the second king of Rome?
18. Who did all of the work in Roman society?
19. What was the only kind of work a Roman citizen could engage in that was not considered degrading?
20. What did Numa Pompilius establish as the basis of the Roman economy?

CHAPTER III

21. Name the three plains on the west coast of Italy, from north to south.
22. What were the Romans and the other people who lived in the plain of Latium called?
23. Three brothers from Rome and three brothers from Alba fought each other. Name them.
24. Where were the Alban hills?

CHAPTER IV

25. What country was Tarquin from?
26. What is the port city of Rome?
27. What is the name for an official Roman fortune teller?
28. On what hill did Tarquin build the temple of Jupiter?
29. Name the king's police force established by Tarquin.
30. Name and describe the symbol of the king's authority.
31. Where were public meetings held?
32. What was the name of the great racetrack built by Tarquin?
33. A "counting of the people" is still called by what Latin word?
34. What was a female fortune teller called?
35. What is the name of the "holy books" bought by Tarquin Superbus, and where were they kept?
36. What does Tarquin Superbus mean?

CHAPTER V

37. Who was the nephew of Tarquin Superbus who pretended to be a simpleton?
38. What event brought about the overthrow of Tarquin Superbus?
39. In what year did Rome change from a monarchy to a republic?
40. In the republic, what was the name of the two rulers who replaced the king?
41. Who said "Down with Tarquin the tyrant, no more kings"?

CHAPTER VI

42. What were the people from Etruria called?
43. What Etruscan king gathered a large army to help Tarquin recapture Rome?
44. Who held back the Etruscan army while the Romans cut down the Sublician bridge?

CHAPTER VII

45. Tell the story of Mucius the Left-Handed.

CHAPTER VIII

46. Where did the Volscians live and what was their capital city?
47. How did the patricians oppress the plebeians?
48. What were the elected representatives of the plebeians called?
49. What could tribunes do to laws they didn't like?
50. When there was a famine what did Coriolanus want the plebeians to give up in exchange for food?
51. Who saved Rome from the traitor Coriolanus?
52. What did Coriolanus say to his mother?

CHAPTER IX

53. What noble family spoke in favor of justice for the plebeians and was hated by the other nobles?
54. What Etruscan city took revenge on the Fabii in a very cowardly way?

CHAPTER X

55. What barbarian tribe living in the mountains east of Rome trapped the Romans in a narrow valley?
56. In times of extreme danger Rome had what kind of leader and for how long?
57. Who was plowing his fields when the Senate came to tell him he had been chosen dictator?
58. How did Cincinnatus humiliate the defeated Aequians?
59. After saving Rome, what did Cincinnatus do that showed he was an "ideal dictator"?

CHAPTER XI

60. What Roman dictator finally defeated the rich city of Veii?
61. What Etruscan city became friends with Rome because Camillus refused a traitorous offer from a wicked schoolmaster?
62. What is the name for the valuable property taken from a defeated enemy?
63. Of what crime was Camillus accused?
64. What did the Romans call the country now known as France?
65. Who was the king of the Gauls when they marched unopposed into Rome?

HISTORY QUESTIONS

66. In what year was the "sack of Rome" by the Gauls?
67. What fortress in Rome was besieged by the Gauls?
68. What alerted the besieged Romans that the Gauls were scaling the steep cliffs of the Capitol?
69. Who was called the second Romulus and the Father of his Country because he drove the Gauls out of Rome?

CHAPTER XII
70. Who killed the giant Gaul who came every day to taunt the Romans?
71. What is the first duty of a soldier?
72. Who ordered his own son executed because of disobedience?

CHAPTER XIII
73. What is the name of the Roman office responsible for the census, tax collection, and public construction?
74. What is the name of the structure Romans built to carry water to cities?
75. What is the name of the most famous Roman road, the "queen of roads"?
76. What Roman censor was called "the greatest of his countrymen in the works of peace"?
77. What did the Romans call the area of southern Italy settled by Greeks?
78. Why did the Greeks consider themselves superior to the Romans?
79. What Greek city in southern Italy attacked a Roman fleet and insulted Roman ambassadors sent to demand satisfaction?
80. Why did the Tarentines laugh at the Roman ambassadors?
81. What did the Roman ambassador say to the Tarentines who threw mud on his toga?
82. What Greek general came from Epirus in Greece to lead the Tarentines against Rome?
83. What new weapon did Pyrrhus use against the Roman soldiers?
84. What is a "Pyrrhic victory"?
85. What saying did the Greeks have about the clever and eloquent speeches of Cineas?
86. Whose speech inspired the Romans to fight instead of accepting the humiliating terms of peace with Tarentum?

PATER NOSTER
THE LORD'S PRAYER

Pater	Noster	Qui es in Caelis	Sanctificetur	Nomen
Pah tair	*Noh stair*	*Kwee es in Chay lees*	*Sahnk tee fee chay' tur*	*Noh men*
Father	Our	Who is in Heaven	Holy (is)	name

Tuum	Adveniat	Regnum	Tuum
Too oom	*Odd vay' nee aht*	*Rayn yoom*	*Too oom*
Your	come	kingdom	your

Fiat	Voluntas	Tua	Sicut	in	Caelo
Fee aht	*Voh loon' tahse*	*Too ah*	*See coot*	*in*	*Chay lo*
be done	will	your	as	in	Heaven

et in Terra	Panem	Nostrum	Cotidianum
et in Tair ah	*Pah nem*	*No stroom*	*Co tee dee ah' noom*
also on Earth	bread	our	daily

Da	Nobis	Hodie	et	Dimitte	Nobis
Dah	*No bees*	*Ho' dee ay*	*et*	*Dee mee tay*	*No beese*
give	to us	this day	and	forgive	us

Debita	Nostra	Sicut	et	Nos	Dimittimus
Day' bee tah	*No strah*	*See coot*	*et*	*Nohs*	*Dee mee' tee moose*
debts	our	as	also	we	forgive

Debitoribus	Nostris	et	Ne	Nos	Inducas
Day bee tor' ee boose	*No strees*	*et*	*Nay*	*Nohs*	*In doo' cahs*
debtors	our	and	not	us	lead

in	Tentationem	Sed	Libera	Nos	A	Malo
in	*Ten taht see oh' nem*	*Said*	*Lee' bay rah*	*Nohs*	*ah*	*mah loh*
into	temptation	but	deliver	us	from	evil

TABLE BLESSING

Benedic,	**Domine,**	**nos**	**et**	**haec**	**Tua**	**dona**
Ben' ay deek	*Doh' mee nay,*	*nohs*	*et*	*hayk*	*Too ah*	*doh nah*
Bless	Oh Lord	us	and	these	your	gifts

quae	**de**	**Tua**	**largitate**	**sumus**	**sumpturi**
kway	*day*	*Too ah*	*lar gee tah' tay*	*soo moose*	*soomp too' ree*
which	from	your	bounty	we are	about to receive

per	**Christum**	**Dominum**	**Nostrum**	**Amen**
pair	*Chree stoom*	*Doh' mee noom*	*Noh stroom*	
through	Christ	Lord	our	Amen

CONVERSATIONAL LATIN

Salvete, amici Latinae.*	*Greetings, friends of Latin.*
Salve, magister / magistra. *(m. / f.)*	*Greetings (hello), teacher.*
Salvete, discipuli.*	*Hello, students.*
Salve, discipule.	*Hello, student.*
Quid est tuum praenomen?	*What is your first name?*
Meum praenomen est...	*My first name is...*
Sede, Sedete.*	*Sit down.*
Surge, surgite.*	*Stand up.*
Oremus.	*Let us pray.*
Quid agis?	*How are you?*
Satis bene.	*Pretty well.*
Vale, magister / magistra.* *(m. / f.)*	*Good bye, teacher.*
Valete, discipuli.	*Good bye, students.*
Gratias tibi ago.	*Thank you.*
Repete, repetite.*	*Repeat.*

* *Salve, sede, surge, vale,* and *repete* are singular imperatives (commands), spoken to one person.

Salvete, sedete, surgite, valete, and *repetite* are plural imperatives (commands), spoken to more than one person.

ADESTE FIDELES
(O COME ALL YE FAITHFUL)

1. Ad-é-ste fi-dé-les, Lae-ti tri-um-phán-tes
2. Can-tet nunc I-o Cho-rus An-ge-ló-rum;

Ve-ní-te, ve-ní-te in Béth-le-hem.
can-tet nunc au-la cae-lé-sti-um.

Na-tum vi-dé-te Re-gem An-ge-ló-rum
Glo-ri-a glo-ria In ex-cél-sis De-o:

Ve-ní-te ad-o-ré-mus, Ve-ní-te ad-o-ré-mus,

Ve-ni-te ad-o-ré-mus Do-mi-num.

O come, all ye faithful	Sing, choirs of angels,	*Refrain*
Joyful and triumphant	Sing in exultation!	O come, let us adore Him
O come ye, O come ye to Bethlehem	Sing, all ye citizens of heav'n above!	O come, let us adore Him
Come and behold Him,	Gloria, gloria	O come, let us adore Him
Born the King of angels!	In excelsis Deo	Christ the lord!

DONA NOBIS PACEM

Do - na no - bis pa - cem. pac - cem.

Do - na no - bis pa - cem.

Do - na no - bis pa - cem.

Do - na no - bis pa - cem.

Do - na no - bis pa - cem.

Do - na no - bis pa - cem.

CHRISTUS VINCIT

With solemnity

Chri - stus vin - cit, Chri - stus re - gnat, Chri - stus, Chri - stus, im - - - pe - rat.

Appendices

LATIN SAYINGS

1. Ora et Labora. — *Pray and work. - St. Benedict*
2. Mater Italiae-Roma — *The mother of Italy - Rome*
3. Caelum et terra — *Heaven and earth*
4. E pluribus unum — *One out of many*
5. Labor omnia vincit. — *Work conquers all. - Virgil*
6. mea culpa — *my fault*
7. Anno Domini, A.D. — *In the year of Our Lord*
8. Semper fidelis — *Always faithful*
9. Senatus Populusque Romanus — *The Senate and People of Rome*
10. stupor mundi — *wonder of the world*
11. ante bellum — *before the war (Civil War)*
12. Excelsior! — *Ever higher!*
13. Sanctus, Sanctus, Sanctus — *Holy, Holy, Holy*
    Dominus Deus Sabaoth — *Lord God of Hosts*
14. Novus ordo seclorum — *New order of the ages*
15. Nunc aut numquam — *Now or never*
16. Veni, vidi, vici. — *I came, I saw, I conquered.*
17. Agnus Dei, qui tollis — *Lamb of God who takes away the*
    peccata mundi. — *sins of the world.*
18. Rident stolidi verba Latina. (Ovid) — *Fools laugh at the Latin language.*
19. Quo vadis? — *Where are you going?*
20. alma mater — *nurturing mother*
21. Pax Romana — *The Roman Peace*
22. Miles Christi sum. — *I am a soldier of Christ.*
23. Vox populi, vox dei — *The voice of the people is the voice of god.*
    (Roman Proverb)
24. Signum crucis — *The sign of the Cross*
25. Et tu, Brute? — *You too, Brutus?*

VERB FORMS
Tense Endings

Present Tense

	S.	Pl.
1st Person	o	mus
2nd Person	s	tis
3rd Person	t	nt

Future Tense

	S.	Pl.
1st P.	bo	bimus
2nd P.	bis	bitis
3rd P.	bit	bunt

Imperfect Tense

	S.	Pl.
1st P.	bam	bamus
2nd P.	bas	batis
3rd P.	bat	bant

First Conjugation

Second Conjugation

S.	Pl.	S.	Pl.

Present Tense

S.	Pl.	S.	Pl.
voco *I call*	vocamus *we call*	moneo *I warn*	monemus *we warn*
vocas *you call*	vocatis *you call*	mones *you warn*	monetis *you warn*
vocat *he, she, it calls*	vocant *they call*	monet *he, she, it warns*	monent *they warn*

Future Tense

S.	Pl.	S.	Pl.
vocabo *I will call*	vocabimus *we will call*	monebo *I will warm*	monebimus *we will warn*
vocabis *you will call*	vocabitis *you will call*	monebis *you will warn*	monebitis *you will warn*
vocabit *he, she, it will call*	vocabunt *they will call*	monebit *he, she, it will warn*	monebunt *they will warn*

Imperfect Tense

S.	Pl.	S.	Pl.
vocabam *I was calling*	vocabamus *we were calling*	monebam *I was warning*	monebamus *we were warning*
vocabas *you were calling*	vocabatis *you were calling*	monebas *you were warning*	monebatis *you were warning*
vocabat *he, she, it was calling*	vocabant *they were calling*	monebat *he, she, it was warning*	monebant *they were warning*

Irregular Verbs

Present tense

		Present tense	
sum *I am*	sumus *we are*	possum *I am able*	possumus *we are able*
es *you are*	estis *you are*	potes *you are able*	potestis *you are able*
est *he is*	sunt *they are*	potest *he, she, it is able*	possunt *they are able*

NOUN & PRONOUN FORMS

NOUN FORMS

First Declension

Case	S.	Pl.	S.	Pl.
Nominative	a	ae	mensa	mensae
Genitive	ae	arum	mensae	mensarum
Dative	ae	is	mensae	mensis
Accusative	am	as	mensam	mensas
Ablative	a	is	mensa	mensis

Second Declension - Masculine

	S.	Pl.	S.	Pl.
Nom.	us	i	servus	servi
Gen.	i	orum	servi	servorum
Dat.	o	is	servo	servis
Acc.	um	os	servum	servos
Abl.	o	is	servo	servis

Second Declension - Neuter

	S.	Pl.	S.	Pl.
Nom.	um	a	donum	dona
Gen.	i	orum	doni	donorum
Dat.	o	is	dono	donis
Acc.	um	a	donum	dona
Abl.	o	is	dono	donis

Pronoun Forms

	First Person		*Second Person*	
	S.	Pl.	S.	Pl.
Nom.	ego	nos	tu	vos
Gen.	mei	nostri, nostrum	tui	vestri, vestrum
Dat.	mihi	nobis	tibi	vobis
Acc.	me	nos	te	vos
Abl.	me	nobis	te	vobis

VOCABULARY INDEX (by Grammar Form)

Latin, *English*   *Lesson*

1st Conjugation verbs

amo, *I love*   *1*
adoro, *I adore*   *5*
ambulo, *I walk*   *5*
appello, *I address*   *17*
clamo, *I shout*   *3*
do, *I give*   *17, 25*
habito, *I live*   *18,25*
judico, *I judge*   *6*
laboro, *I work*   *1*
laudo, *I praise*   *1*
lavo, *I wash*   *18, 25*

libero, *I free*   *5*
narro, *I tell*   *17,25*
navigo, *I sail*   *2*
occupo, *I seize*   *6*
oro, *I pray*   *1*
paro, *I prepare*   *2*
porto, *I carry*   *1*
pugno, *I fight*   *6*
specto, *I look at*   *2*
supero, *I conquer*   *3*
voco, *I call*   *3*

2nd Conjugation Verbs

debeo, *I ought, owe*   *16*
doceo, *I teach*   *16*
habeo, *I have*   *16*
jubeo, *I order*   *16*
moneo, *I warn*   *16*
moveo, *I move*   *16*
prohibeo, *I prevent*   *16*
sedeo, *I sit*   *17*
terreo, *I frighten*   *16*
timeo, *I fear*   *16*
video, *I see*   *16*

1st Declension Nouns

aqua, *water*   *2*
aquila, *eagle*   *9*
auriga, *charioteer*   *23*
aurora, *dawn*   *18*
cena, *dinner*   *18*
corona, *crown*   *9*
culpa, *fault*   *6*
ecclesia, *church*   *9*
fama, *fame*   *8, 22*
femina, *woman*   *5*
fenestra, *window*   *18*
filia, *daughter* *5*
fortuna, *luck*   *3*
fuga, *flight*   *6*
Gallia, *Gaul*   *3*
gloria, *glory*   *2*

gratia, *grace*   *8*
herba, *plant*   *3*
Hispania, *Spain*   *6*
hora, *hour*   *8, 22*
injuria, *injury*   *17*
insula, *island*   *17*
ira, *anger*   *7, 23*
Italia, *Italy*   *2*
lingua, *language*   *3, 20*
luna, *moon*   *6*
Maria, *Mary*   *6*
memoria, *memory*   *2*
mensa, *table*   *5, 20*
mora, *delay*   *9*
nauta, *sailor*   *3*

patria, *country*   *5, 24*
pecunia, *money*   *9, 20*
puella, *girl*   *5*
pugna, *fight*   *18*
regina, *queen*   *5*
Roma, *Rome*   *2*
silva, *forest*   *6, 23*
stella, *star*   *7*
terra, *land*   *3*
toga, *toga*   *5*
unda, *wave*   *6*
ursa, *bear*   *7*
via, *road*   *3*
victoria, *victory*   *2*
vita, *life*   *2*

2nd Declension nouns – Masculine

agnus, *lamb*   *17*
amicus, *friend*   *7*
animus, *spirit*   *9*
annus, *year*   *7*
barbarus, *barbarian*   *10*
campus, *field*   *10*
capillus, *hair*   *10*

cibus, *food*   *10*
Christus, *Christ*   *8*
Deus, *God*   *8*
discipulus, *student*   *8*
dominus, *lord*   *7*
equus, *horse*   *10*
filius, *son*   *7*

gladius, *sword*   *9*
hortus, *garden*   *18*
legatus, *envoy*   *8*
locus, *place*   *10*
ludus, *school*   *9*
mundus, *world*   *10*
murus, *wall*   *9*

nimbus, *cloud*   *18*
nuntius, *message*   *10*
oculus, *eye*   *17*
populus, *people*   *9*
servus, *slave*   *7*
socius, *ally*   *10*
ventus, *wind*   *10*

VOCABULARY INDEX (by Grammar Form)

Latin, *English* *Lesson*

2nd Declension nouns – Neuter

auxilium, *help* *12*
bellum, *war* *11*
caelum, *heavenn* *12*
debitum, *debt* *12*
donum, *gift* *11*
forum, *forum* *12*
frumentum, *grain* *11*
gaudium, *joy* *12*
imperium, *command* *11*
oppidum, *town* *11*

peccatum, *sin* *12*
praemium, *reward* *12, 24*
proelium, *battle* *11, 24*
regnum, *kingdom* *11*
signum, *sign, standard* *11*
telum, *weapon* *11*
tergum, *back* *12*
vallum, *wall* *12*
verbum, *word* *11*
vinum, *wine* *12*

3rd Declension nouns

Caesar, Caesaris, *Caesar* *21*
canis, canis, *dog* *22*
caput, capitis, *head* *21*
centurio, centurionis, *centurion* *22*
civitas, civitatis, *state* *22*
collis, collis, *hill* *24*
corpus, corporis, *body* *22*
crux, crucis, *cross* *24*
dolor, doloris, *sorrow* *25*
flumen, fluminis, *river* *25*
frater, fratris, *brother* *20*
gens, gentis, *tribe* *25*
homo, hominis, *man* *23*
hostis, hostis, *enemy* *21*
ignis, ignis, *fire* *21*
imperator, imperatoris, *commander* *23*
legio, legionis, *legion* *23*
lex, legis, *law* *20*
lux, lucis, *light* *21*

mater, matris, *mother* *20*
miles, militis, *soldier* *22*
mons, montis, *mountain* *22*
mors, mortis, *death* *25*
navis, navis, *ship* *24*
nomen, nominis, *name* *22*
nox, noctis, *night* *24*
ordo, ordinis, *order* *21*
pars, partis, *part* *25*
pater, patris, *father* *20*
pax, pacis, *peace* *21*
pons, pontis, *bridge* *21*
rex, regis, *king* *20*
soror, sororis, *sister* *22*
tempus, temporis, *time* *21*
urbs, urbis, *city* *23*
veritas, veritatis, *truth* *21*
virtus, virtutis, *courage* *24*
vox, vocis, *voice* *23*

Adjectives

aeternus, *eternal* *14*
altus, *high, deep* *13*
bonus, *good* *13*
certus, *certain* *14*
longus, *long* *13*
magnus, *large* *13*
malus, *bad* *13*

meus, *my* *17*
multus, *much* *13*
novus, *new* *14*
parvus, *small* *13*
plenus, *full* *13*
primus, *first* *14*
proximus, *near* *14*

sanctus, *holy* *13*
secundus, *second* *14*
solus, *alone* *14*
summus, *highest* *14*
tertius, *third* *14*
totus, *whole* *14, 23*
tutus, *safe* *13, 24*
tuus, *your* *17*

VOCABULARY INDEX(by Grammar Form)

Latin, *English*   Lesson

Adverbs
bene, *well*   15
clam, *secretly*   15
non, *not*   15
numquam, *never*   15
nunc, *now*   15
saepe, *often*   8
semper, *always*   8

Prepositions
ante, *before*   7
contra, *against*   15
ex, *out of*   15
inter, *between*   15
post, *after*   7
sub, *under*   15
supra, *over*   15

Constellations
aquarius, *water carrier*   19
aries, *ram*   19
cancer, *crab*   19
capricorn, *goat*   19
gemini, *the twins*   19
leo, *lion*   19
libra, *scales*   19
pisces, *fish*   19
sagittarius, *archer*   19
scorpio, *scorpion*   19
taurus, *bull*   19
virgo, *virgin*   19

Numbers
unus, *one*   4
duo, *two*   4
tres, *three*   4
quattuor, *four*   4
quinque, *five*   4
sex, *six*   4
septem, *seven*   4
octo, *eight*   4
novem, *nine*   4
decem, *ten*   4
centum, *hundred*   4
mille, *thousand*   4

Other words
Jesus   8
sicut, *as*   18, 23
et, *and*   20

VOCABULARY INDEX (by Grammar Form)

Latin	English	Derivatives
adoro	I adore	*adoration*
aeternus -a -um	eternal, everlasting	*eternity*
agnus -i	lamb	
altus -a -um	high, deep	*altitude, altar*
ambulo	I walk	*ambulance*
amicus -i	friend	*amicable*
amo	I like, I love	*amorous, amateur*
animus -i	mind, spirit	*animated, animal*
annus -i	year	*annual, annals, anniversary*
ante	before	*antique*
appello	I speak to, I address	*appeal, appellation*
aqua -ae	water	*aquarium, aqueduct*
aquarius -i	water-carrier	
aquila -ae	eagle	*aquiline*
aries -etis	ram	
auriga -ae	charioteer	
aurora -ae	dawn	*aurora borealis*
auxilium -i	help, aid	*auxiliary*
barbarus -i	barbarian	*barbaric*
bellum -i	war	*bellicose, belligerent, rebel*
bene	well	*benefit, benevolent*
bonus -a -um	good	*bonbon, bonny*
caelum -i	sky, heaven	*celestial*
Caesar -aris	Caesar	*tsar, czar*
campus -i	field, plain	*camp*
cancer -cri	crab	
canis canis	dog	*canine*
capillus -i	hair	*capillary*
capricornus -i	Capricorn	
caput -itis	head	*Capitol, capital, capitalize*
cena -ae	dinner	
centum	hundred	*cent, century, percent, centennial, centigrade*
centurio -onis	centurion	
certus -a -um	certain, sure	*certainly*
Christus -i	Christ	
cibus -i	food	*ciborium*
civitas -atis	state	*civil, civility, city, citizen, civilization*
clam	secretly	*clandestine*
clamo	I shout	*clamor, clamorous, exclamation, claim*
collis collis	hill	
contra	against	*contradict, contrary, contrast*
corona -ae	crown	*coronation*
corpus -oris	body	*corporal, corpse, corps, corporation*
crux crucis	cross	*crucifix, crucifixion, crucial*
culpa -ae	fault, crime	*culprit, culpable*
debeo	I owe, I ought	*debt, debtor, duty*
debitum -i	debt, trespass	*debit*

VOCABULARY INDEX *(by Grammar Form)*

Latin	English	Derivatives
decem	ten	*December*
Deus -i	God	*deity*
discipulus -i	student	*disciple*
do	I give	*donate*
doceo	I teach	*docile, document, doctrine, indoctrinate*
dolor -oris	pain, sorrow	*dolorous, Via Dolorosa*
dominus -i	lord, master	*dominate, dominion*
donum -i	gift	*donate, donation, donor*
duo	two	*duet, dual, duo, duel*
ecclesia -ae	church	*Ecclesiastes, ecclesiastical*
equus -i	horse	*equine, equestrian*
et	and	*etcetera*
ex	out of	*exit, extra*
fama -ae	fame, rumor	*famous, infamous*
femina -ae	woman	*feminine, female*
fenestra -ae	window	
filia -ae	daughter	*filial*
filius -i	son	*filial*
flumen -inis	river	*fluid, fluent*
fortuna -ae	fortune, chance	*fortune, fortunate*
forum -i	forum	
frater fratris	brother	*fraternal, fraternity*
frumentum -i	wheat, grain	
fuga -ae	flight	*fugitive, refugee, fugue*
Gallia -ae	Gaul	*Gallic*
gaudium -i	joy	*gaudy*
geminus -i	twin	
gens gentis	tribe	*genitive, progeny, generate, gender*
gladius -i	short sword	*gladiator, gladiola*
gloria -ae	glory	*glorious, glorify*
gratia -ae	grace	*gracious, gratitude*
habeo	I have	*habit*
habito	I live in, I inhabit	*inhabit, habitation*
herba -ae	grass	*herb, herbal, herbivore*
Hispania -ae	Spain	*Hispanic*
homo -inis	man, person	*homicide, homo sapiens*
hora -ae	hour	*horoscope*
hortus -i	garden	*horticulture*
hostis hostis	enemy	*hostile, hostility*
ignis ignis	fire	*ignite, ignition, igneous*
imperator -oris	general, commander	*imperative*
imperium -i	command, empire	*imperial, emperor, empire, imperious*
injuria -ae	injury	*injurious*
insula -ae	island	*insulate, insular*
inter	between	*interior, intermission, intergalactic, interlude*
ira -ae	anger	*ire, irate*
Italia -ae	Italy	*italics*
Jesus	Jesus	

VOCABULARY INDEX (by Grammar Form)

Latin	English	Derivatives
jubeo	I order, I command	
judico	I judge, I consider	*judiciary, justice*
laboro	I work	*laborious, laboratory*
laudo	I praise	*laud, laudable*
lavo	I wash	*lava, lavatory, lave*
legatus -i	lieutenant, envoy	*delegate*
legio -onis	legion	*legionary*
leo -onis	lion	*leonine*
lex legis	law	*legal, legislature*
libero	I free	*liberate, liberal, liberty*
libra -ae	scales	
lingua -ae	tongue, language	*language, bilingual, linguistic*
locus -i	place	*local, location*
longus -a -um	long	*longitude*
ludus -i	game, sport, school	*ludicrous*
luna -ae	moon	*lunar, lunacy, lunatic*
lux lucis	light	*lucid, Lucifer*
magnus -a -um	large, great	*magnify, magnificent*
malus -a -um	bad	*malady, maladjusted, malice, dismal*
Maria -ae	Mary	*Mary*
mater matris	mother	*maternal, matrimony*
memoria -ae	memory	*memorial, memorize*
mensa -ae	table	*mesa*
meus -a -um	my	
miles -itis	soldier	*military, militia*
mille	thousand	*mile, million, milligram, millenium*
moneo	I warn, I advise	*monitor, admonish*
mons montis	mountain	*mount*
mora -ae	delay	*moratorium*
mors mortis	death	*mortal, mortality, immortal*
moveo	I move	*movie, remove, move, movable*
multus -a -um	much, many	*multiply, multitude*
mundus -i	world, mankind	*mundane*
murus -i	wall	*mural*
narro	I tell	*narrator*
nauta -ae	sailor	*nautilus, nautical*
navigo	I sail, navigate	*navigate, navigation*
navis navis	ship	*navy, naval*
nimbus -i	cloud	
nomen -inis	name	*nominate, noun, nominative*
non	not	*nonsense*
novem	nine	*November*
novus -a -um	new	*novel, novice, innovate, renovate*
nox noctis	night	*nocturnal, equinox*
numquam	never	
nunc	now	
nuntius -i	messenger, message	*announce, pronounce*
occupo	I seize	*occupy, occupation*

VOCABULARY INDEX (by Grammar Form)

Latin	English	Derivatives
octo	eight	*October*
oculus -i	eye	*ocular, binocular*
oppidum -i	town	
ordo ordinis	rank	*order, ordain*
oro	I pray, I give a speech	*oratory, orator*
paro	I prepare	*preparation*
pars partis	part	*particle, particular, partial*
parvus -a -um	small, insignificant	
pater patris	father	*paternal, patrician*
patria -ae	country, fatherland	*patriot, patriotic*
pax pacis	peace	*pacify, pacific, pacifier*
peccatum -i	mistake, sin	*impeccable, peccadillo*
pecunia -ae	money, wealth	*pecuniary, peculiar (from **pecus**, cow)*
pisces (piscis -is)	fish (pl.)	
plenus -a -um	full	*plenary, plenty, plentiful*
pons pontis	bridge	*pontoon*
populus -i	people	*population, popular*
porto	I carry	*portable, transport, export, import*
post	after	*posterior, posterity*
praemium -i	reward	*premium*
primus -a -um	first	*primary, prime*
proelium -i	battle	
prohibeo	I prevent	*prohibit*
proximus -a -um	nearest, next	*proximity, approximate*
summus -a -um	highest, greatest	*summit, sum*
puella -ae	girl	
pugna -ae	fight	*pugnacious, repugnant*
pugno	I fight	*pugnacious*
quattuor	four	*quart, quarter, quartet (from **quartus**, fourth)*
quinque	five	*quintuplets (from **quintus**, fifth)*
regina -ae	queen	
regnum -i	kingdom	
rex regis	king	*regal, Tyrannosaurus Rex*
Roma -ae	Rome	*Roman*
saepe	often	
sagittarius -i	archer	
sanctus -a -um	holy, saintly	*sanctify, sanctification, sanctuary*
scorpio -onis	scorpion	
secundus -a -um	second	*secondary, second*
sedeo	I sit	*sedentary, sediment, sedate*
semper	always	
septem	seven	*September*
servus -i	slave	*service, servant, servile*
sex	six	*sextet*
sicut	as	
signum -i	sign, standard	*signal, signature, insignia, design*
silva -ae	forest	*sylvan, Pennsylvania, Transylvania*
socius -i	ally, comrade	*social, society*

VOCABULARY INDEX (by Grammar Form)

Latin	English	Derivatives
solus -a -um	alone, only	*solitary, solitude, solo*
soror -oris	sister	*sorority*
specto	I look at	*spectacle, inspect, spectator, spectacular*
stella -ae	star	*stellar*
sub	under	*submarine, subway*
supero	I overcome, I conquer	*superior*
supra	above	*supranational*
taurus -i	bull	
telum -i	weapon	
tempus -oris	time	*temporal, tempo, tense*
tergum -i	back	
terra -ae	land, earth	*terrestrial, terrain, territory, Mediterranean*
terreo	I frighten	*terrify*
tertius -a -um	third	*tertiary*
timeo	I fear	*timid, intimidate*
toga -ae	toga	*toga*
totus -a -um	whole	*total*
tres	three	*trio, triangle*
tutus -a -um	safe	
tuus -a -um	your (singular)	
unda -ae	wave	*undulate, inundate*
unus	one	*unity, universe, union, unit, unique*
urbs urbis	city, Rome	*urban, suburb*
ursa -ae	(she-) bear	*Ursa Major, Ursa Minor*
vallum -i	wall, rampart	
ventus -i	wind	*vent, ventilate*
verbum -i	word	*verbal, verbose, verb*
veritas -atis	truth	*verity, verify, very*
via -ae	road, way	*viaduct, via*
victoria -ae	victory	*victorious*
video	I see	*evident, vision, video*
vinum -i	wine	*vine, vineyard*
virgo -inis	maiden, virgin	
virtus -utis	virtue, courage	*virtuous, virtue*
vita -ae	life	*vital, vitamin*
voco	I call	*vocal, vocation*
vox vocis	voice	*vocal, vocation*